# Sharing the Environment

Written by Anna Porter

Series Consultant: Linda Hoyt

**WorldWise**
Content-based Learning

# Contents

# Chapter 1

# People create problems; people create solutions

## The problem: Animals and their habitats at risk

What do the animals in these pictures have in common?

They are all listed as **endangered species**, which means there are so few of them in the world that they may become **extinct** in the wild in our lifetime. These animals have become endangered because their **habitat** has been lost or changed so much that they cannot survive as a species.

All animals need food, water, shelter and space to survive and produce young. An animal's natural habitat is an area that provides for all these needs.

Like animals, people also need food, water, shelter and space. The human **population** of the world is increasing all the time.

**Did you know?**

In the past 50 years, the world population nearly doubled. Our planet now has to support and feed about 7.5 billion people.

Over time, the needs of people have destroyed animal habitats in many ways:

- Animal habitats have been made into farmland to grow food for people.
- Land has been cleared to make space for houses.
- Trees have been cut down to provide lumber to build houses.
- Dams and **irrigation** channels have been built to provide water for people and crops, and this has changed rivers and streams.

It is important to balance the needs of people and animals so that animals are able to survive in their natural habitats. Many people, groups and governments have become very concerned about the problem of habitat destruction around the world and about the number of animals this has endangered.

# The solution: Finding a balance

Around the world people have recognised that many animals are endangered. They have formed organisations to help protect endangered animals. One of these organisations publishes the Red List, which is a list of animals at high risk of becoming extinct.

The Global 200 map shows more than 200 land, freshwater and **marine** habitats around the world that people need to protect if endangered species are to survive.

This map was developed by scientists from the World Wildlife Fund (WWF).

**Did you know?**

The Red List, which is published by the International Union for Conservation of Nature and Natural Resources, labels endangered animals, according to their level of risk.

- Extinct: no longer existing
- Extinct in the wild: no longer existing in the wild
- Critically endangered: at extremely high risk of becoming extinct
- Endangered: at risk of becoming extinct
- Vulnerable: threatened but not quite endangered
- Near threatened: may be considered threatened in the near future.

Yosemite National Park, USA, is a World Heritage Site.

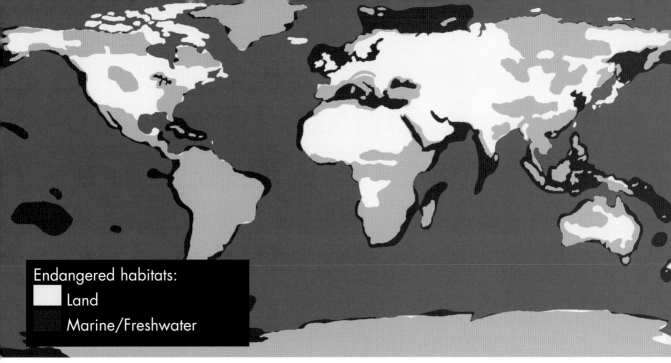

Endangered habitats:
■ Land
▨ Marine/Freshwater

There are many ways that people take action to protect animals. Some areas of natural habitat have been set aside as **conservation** areas, such as national parks or **World Heritage Sites**. Other areas have been replanted with native plants to re-create a habitat.

Scientists have set up programs in zoos, **sanctuaries** and research centres where endangered animals can breed, so their numbers can be increased before they are returned to the wild. This is called **captive breeding**.

Also, people now understand that some **pesticides** used on crops to kill insect pests have also killed large numbers of birds. Many people no longer use these dangerous chemicals on crops.

This book looks at endangered animals in several habitats and outlines ways that people have tried to save these animals.

National parks help educate people about the environment.

7

# Chapter 2

# Forest habitats

Clearing forest habitat

In the past 25 years, more than 130 million hectares of forests were destroyed around the world. Most of this land has been made into farmland. As a result, pandas, lemurs and condors have lost their natural forest **habitats**, so people have been working to save them.

# Giant pandas

Giant pandas belong to the bear family, which includes grizzly bears and polar bears. They live in one small habitat in a part of China, and mainly eat one type of food – bamboo. The pandas live high up in the mountains where there are bamboo forests. They spend up to 16 hours a day eating, and eat about 15 kilograms of bamboo each day. Each giant panda lives alone for most of the year, and needs a large **territory** of its own, because it has to eat so much bamboo every day to remain healthy.

### Think about ...

Scientists predict that climate change could mean that one-third of the habitat essential to the long-term survival of giant pandas in China could disappear.

## Problems of habitat destruction

Giant pandas became **endangered** because much of the bamboo they eat was being cleared for farming and housing. Because of this, many giant pandas have starved to death, making them one of the rarest of all **mammals**.

## Great news!

The people of China have been working hard to try to save the panda. In 2016, their hard work was rewarded when the International Union for Conservation of Nature downgraded the status of giant pandas from endangered to vulnerable. This is because numbers in the wild have increased from 1,596 in 2004 to 1,864 in 2016.

Bamboo

| Year | Number of giant pandas found in the wild |
|------|------------------------------------------|
| 1976 | 1,000 |
| 1985 | 800–1,200 |
| 1987 | 1,000 |
| 1994 | 1,200 |
| 1995 | 1,000 |
| 2004 | 1,596 |
| 2016 | 1,864 |

This success story is a result of the work done by the Chinese government, the World Wildlife Fund (WWF), and zoos. The government passed laws to protect giant panda habitats as nature reserves and planted bamboo forests to extend the reserves. These reserves now cover more than 1.5 million hectares.

A newborn panda at a captive breeding centre

The Chinese government lent giant pandas to zoos such as the Smithsonian's National Zoo and San Diego Zoo in the United States. At these zoos, scientists have set up captive breeding centres. One of the pandas, Bai Yun, gave birth to a female cub named Hua Mei in 1999. This cub was returned to China as part of the giant panda breeding and conservation program. Hua Mei has now given birth to 11 of her own cubs.

## Other endangered bears

▲ Grizzly bear (in parts of Canada)

▲ Malayan sun bear

### Find out more

Why does the WWF use the giant panda in its logo?

# Lemurs

Lemurs are a type of primate only found wild on the island of Madagascar, off the east coast of Africa. Over the past 2,000 years, people on this island have cleared the natural forest to make farmland. Today, only about 10 per cent of the original **vegetation** remains.

There are now 17 million people living on this small island, and the population is increasing quickly. As a result, one-third of the lemur species on the island has become extinct and several others are almost extinct. Many countries are working together to save these animals. Different species of lemur are now bred and raised in **captivity** before being returned to the wild in Madagascar.

**? Did you know?**

There are more than 90 species of lemur, and all of them are classified as either endangered or vulnerable on the Red List.

This land in Madagascar has been cleared for housing and farming.

# Saving the lemurs of Madagascar

I am a volunteer with the Duke Lemur Center at Duke University in North Carolina, in the United States. I study biology at the university, and my special study is lemurs.

I started out as a volunteer tour guide at the Lemur Center, and I am now a volunteer animal technician. I clean the enclosures and feed the animals.

Next year, I am going to do field research in Madagascar. I will be monitoring the numbers of the black-and-white ruffed lemurs and their young. This is the only species of lemur from our captive breeding program ever to be introduced back to the wild, so I am very excited.

I will also be working at a zoo, where I will help teach the local people about **reforesting** the island's original habitat to conserve the lemurs. We will also be talking about **ecotourism**, where people are encouraged to visit natural habitats, without damaging them. In this way, the local people can share the environment with the lemurs.

## Did you know?

Primates are a group of mammals that include monkeys, apes and humans.

## Other endangered primates

- Aye-aye
- Central American squirrel monkey
- Golden-headed lion tamarin
- Eastern lowland gorilla
- Zanzibar red colobus

▼ White-bellied spider monkey

▼ Western lowland gorilla

▼ Lion-tailed macaque

# Cliffs for the Californian condor

Some people in California build houses on cliff tops for the views. This has not been good for animals that live and find food on the cliffs.

For many years the largest North American bird, the Californian condor, has been pushed out of its natural forest habitat by people. These giant birds of prey have a wingspan of more than three metres and weigh up to 11 kilograms. They need high cliffs or mountains with caves or ledges for nesting, and large open spaces for flying.

The numbers of this bird declined until it was near extinction, and it was placed on the Californian endangered species list in 1971. By the early 1980s, it was clear that captive breeding was the only chance the Californian condor had to survive.

Scientists at the San Diego Zoo and the Los Angeles Zoo set up breeding centres for the condor. They captured the last 26 condors in the wild and took them to the centres for breeding.

In 1988, these condors were bred successfully for the first time and by late 1995, the population had grown to 103.

In January 1992, some of these young condors were released into the California wilds. By December 2015 there were 435 living condors, about 265 of them living in the wild in California.

## Did you know?

Condors can fly 8,000 metres above the earth to look down for prey. This is nearly as high as planes that fly at 10,000 metres. To do this, condors use their giant wings to take off from cliffs and then search for rising air currents to take them up high. The tips of their wings spread out like fingers to help them glide better.

# Saving the peregrine falcon

During the 1950s and 1960s, the peregrine falcon became endangered because of the overuse of **pesticides** on crops. When these birds ate **prey** that had been poisoned by pesticides such as DDT, their eggshells became thin and less able to hatch into young falcons. In several parts of the world, this species of falcon was almost wiped out by these pesticides; therefore it was listed as endangered.

People **lobbied** governments to ban the use of DDT, and now the numbers of peregrine falcons have built up so that they are no longer endangered.

## Other endangered birds of prey
- White-breasted sea eagle
- Red-tailed hawk
- Philippine eagle
- Mauritius kestrel

▼ Barred owl

# Chapter 3

# Grassland habitats

Grassland is land where there is much more grass or grass-like plants than trees and shrubs. Over time, people have used grasslands around the world to grow crops and to feed herds of farming animals. This has meant that some **species**, such as the wild Mongolian Przewalski (say: *pris-vaal-ski*) horse, the white rhinoceros, the black rhinoceros and the American bison, have almost become **extinct**.

As part of **conservation** efforts to save these animals, some countries have developed open-range wildlife **refuges** and zoos, where these animals breed in **captivity** and roam over large areas of land as they would in their natural **habitat**.

The Przewalski horse

**Did you know?**

The Przewalski horse is Mongolia's national symbol. It was named after a Russian colonel, Nikolai Przewalski.

## The Przewalski horse

I am a zookeeper at the Western Plains Zoo at Dubbo in Australia. I came to work here because I believe open-range zoos like this are important to the conservation of **endangered** animals. People are destroying the natural habitats of these animals, so they cannot get the food they need and are in danger of becoming extinct. The zoos create a habitat for the animals, and have **captive breeding** programs to increase their numbers. They then release them back into the wild.

One of our breeding programs is for the Przewalski horse from Mongolia. This horse was able to survive the extreme temperatures – both hot and cold – in Mongolia.

Over time, people began raising other livestock such as sheep, goats, cattle and camels, and as the natural habitat of the wild horses disappeared, they gradually became extinct in the wild in 1968. This horse has been saved from total extinction through captive breeding in zoos, such as the one in Dubbo, and another at the Wild Animal Park, part of the San Diego Zoo in California.

In June 1995, five Przewalski horses were reintroduced into the wild in Mongolia. To protect them and their young, a 9,700-hectare area of grassland has been turned into the Hustai National Park and is closed off to other livestock. This means these horses now have enough to eat because they do not compete for food with other grazing animals.

17

# Rhinoceroses

By the middle of last century, the number of rhinoceroses in parts of Africa had declined seriously because they had been hunted for their horns. In 1960, "Operation Rhino" was introduced in South Africa. White rhinoceroses were caught and taken to **sanctuaries**. This has meant that their numbers have increased from 500 in 1960 to more than 20,000 today.

The black rhinoceros is now the most endangered rhinoceros species. Open-range zoos in some countries now have captive breeding programs for the black rhinoceros. They hope to be able to release these animals back into the wild in Africa.

### Did you know?

The Western Plains Zoo in Australia has three endangered species of rhinoceros: the black, white and greater one-horned rhinoceros. The black rhinoceros has been successfully bred at this zoo. The zoo recently received five white rhinoceroses from South Africa for its breeding program, and a calf has already been born.

▲ White rhinoceros

▼ Black rhinoceros

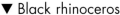

# Gouldian finches

Gouldian finches are beautifully coloured birds that need native grasslands as they depend on seeds from the grasses for food. Fewer than 2,500 Gouldian finches remain in the wild and they are one of Australia's most endangered birds.

A lot of native grassland in Australia has been turned into pasture for cattle and sheep or used for crops. Grassland has also been removed to make way for roads, cities and towns. Plants introduced from other countries have become weeds and overtaken the native grasses. Animals introduced from other countries such as donkeys eat the grasses.

A conservation organisation, the Australian Wildlife Conservancy, in cooperation with the Australian government, has set aside a large open range area of about 360,000 hectares at Mornington Wildlife Sanctuary in the Kimberley region of Western Australia to protect one of the largest remaining populations of the Gouldian finch.

Scientists study the Gouldian finch at the research centre at Mornington and visitors are encouraged to note the location of the birds they see within the sanctuary.

**Did you know?**

Today, only 1 per cent of native grasslands survive in Australia. Grasslands have become one of the most threatened Australian habitats.

More than 80 reptiles and amphibians, over 30 species of mammals as well as 189 bird species are protected at Mornington Wildlife Sanctuary.

# Butterflies

Many tiny creatures are at risk of extinction when grasslands and other **vegetation** are cleared. There are about 17,000 species of butterflies around the world, and some of them lay their eggs on only one kind of plant, which will also feed their **larvae**. People now realise that they need to protect particular plant habitats or regrow these plants to save certain butterflies.

## The Karner blue butterfly

The tiny Karner blue butterfly has now become a symbol of butterfly conservation in the United States. This butterfly can survive only if it has wild lupine plants on which to lay its eggs, because it feeds on the nectar of the flowers, and its larvae only eat the leaves of this plant.

**Did you know?**

Thirty years ago it was estimated that there were 2,000 to 3,000 Karner blue butterflies in the Concord Pine Barrens area of New Hampshire. By 1995, that number had plummeted to fewer than 50 because of the destruction of wild lupine habitat in the area.

Over the years, housing, roads and industrial and farming developments have destroyed the habitat needed by wild lupine and the Karner blue butterfly. The Karner blue can now be found in only a few states and was listed as an endangered species in 1992.

Left, a Karner blue butterfly; right, Karner blue larvae feeding on wild lupine

A conservation plan was developed by Roger Williams Park Zoo on Rhode Island with schools and groups in Concord, New Hampshire. This has restored the habitat for the butterfly and increased its numbers. Other states, such as Wisconsin and Illinois, also have conservation programs for this butterfly. Similar plans to replant habitat, breed and reintroduce certain species of butterflies will now be used to help the other 21 endangered butterfly species throughout the United States.

# Butterfly facts

The world's largest butterfly is the Queen Alexandra birdwing butterfly from Papua New Guinea, which has a wingspan of 30 centimetres. It is an endangered species.

The Karner blue butterfly is one of the smallest butterflies, with a wingspan of about 2.5 centimetres. As small, weak fliers, most Karner blues never travel more than about 200 metres from their home lupine patch. They were first described as a species in the town of Karner, in New York State, in the United States, and were named after this town.

Queen Alexandra birdwing butterfly

## Other endangered butterflies

- Myrtle's silverspot butterfly
- Lange's metalmark butterfly
- Taylor's checkerspot butterfly
- ▼ The Schaus swallowtail butterfly

## Comparative size of butterflies

Queen Alexandra
wingspan:
30 cm

Karner blue
wingspan:
2.5 cm

## Bringing back butterflies

Hi, my name is Kayla. Our school is part of a project to bring back the beautiful Karner blue butterfly, New Hampshire's official state butterfly. In our classroom, we have been growing wild lupine seedlings that we got from the greenhouse at the Roger Williams Park Zoo. In April, we transplanted the lupines at the Karner Blue Butterfly Conservation Easement, where zoo workers are restoring a habitat for wild lupines to grow again.

Last week, we visited the captive butterfly centre at the zoo to watch hundreds of Karner larvae munching on wild lupine plants. Today, we saw the Karner blue butterflies on the wild lupine that we had grown and transplanted last year. It was so exciting and rewarding. We have now made pamphlets that tell others what to do to help bring back this butterfly and share its environment.

# Help Save Butterflies

## What you can do!

Buy native seeds from a nursery or butterfly Conservation group.

Seeds

Plant native plants so that butterfly larvae have food to eat.

Plant wild flowers to provide nectar for butterflies.

Protect native plants that grow on the roadside.

Do not use fertilisers or pesticides, as they can destroy native grasses.

Remove grass clippings and leaves that may cover native plants.

Try not to step on small native plants as there may be butterfly eggs or larvae on them.

Make "keep off" posters for areas where native plants grow.

Keep off

# Chapter 4

# Coastal and marine habitats

Nearly 40 per cent of the total human **population** of the world lives within about 60 kilometres of the coastline. Because people have used the land along the coast for housing, roads, tourism and other industries, the **habitats** of some **marine** animals have been destroyed.

## Marine turtles

Marine turtles need quiet beaches to dig out nests, to lay eggs and to produce young. When the young have hatched, they cross the beach to get to the sea. People and their vehicles trample many of the nesting sites. Lights from houses, cars and trucks can attract **hatchlings** so that they lose their way when trying to get across the beach to the sea. Instead of quickly finding the ocean, these hatchlings may be eaten by **predators** or die from the heat of the sun if they get stranded.

Marine turtles feed in areas close to the coast such as coral reefs, mangrove forests and seagrass beds. These areas are often damaged or destroyed by polluted run-off from the land. It is also estimated that thousands of marine turtles are caught in shrimp nets.

| Species of turtles | Red List status |
|---|---|
| Atlantic (Kemp's) ridley | Endangered |
| Flatback | Critically endangered |
| Green sea | Endangered |
| Hawksbill | Endangered |
| Leatherback sea | Critically endangered |
| Loggerhead sea | Endangered |
| Pacific (olive) ridley | Endangered |

Many marine turtles are killed so turtle products can be made and traded. As a result, all seven **species** of marine turtles are now listed as **endangered**.

## Conservation action

Countries around the world need to cooperate to protect these turtles. The World Wildlife Fund (WWF) is working to conserve marine turtles by

- establishing protected areas around nesting beaches;
- tagging turtles and tracking their activities so scientists can learn of the factors that may lead to their deaths;
- promoting awareness and **ecotourism** at marine turtle sites, so that local communities become involved in protecting turtles and their nests;
- lobbying for shrimp nets to have special devices on them that let the turtles out without losing the shrimp.

# Sea otters

The California or southern sea otter is one of three species of sea otters in the world. It was once found along California's entire coastline, but numbers have declined for several reasons, including

- the otters have been hunted for their **pelts**;
- oil spills leave a coating of oil on sea otters' fur, making it difficult for them to keep warm, which can cause them to die;
- when they are relocated to other parts of the ocean, they have difficulty adapting to their new habitat;
- they are easily caught in fishing nets and die;
- they feed on shellfish that fisheries harvest, so fisherpeople have sometimes shot the otters, or chased them away.

Even worse, sea otters are dying from disease and pollution in these coastal waters. Deadly chemicals build up in the bodies of sea urchins, mussels, clams and other shellfish, which are then eaten by sea otters.

Today, there are about 2,500 southern sea otters off the coast of California, and these sea otters are now listed as threatened under the US Endangered Species Act.

The sea otter is an important species in the kelp forest **ecosystem**. Kelp forests are underwater forests of seaweed that provide food and shelter for large numbers of fish and shellfish. They also protect coastlines from wave action that **erodes** the beaches. Sea otters prey on sea urchins and other kelp grazers and keep their numbers in check so not too much kelp is eaten.

If the number of sea otters continues to decline, the number of sea urchins will rise. The sea urchins will destroy more of the marine kelp habitat, and there will not be enough food for fish and shellfish.

▲ Kelp forest

▼ Sea urchin

### Did you know?

The sea otter has the thickest fur in the animal kingdom, but if an otter's fur gets coated with oil or any other substance, the otter can easily die from cold. This is because the sea otter, unlike other marine mammals, does not have a layer of fat under its skin to help keep it warm.

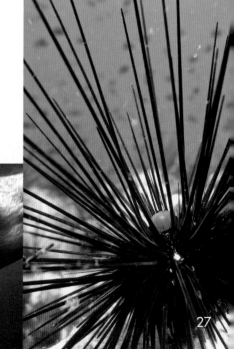

## Conservation attempts

There were attempts to create a no-otter zone along the Southern California coast and to relocate sea otters. This was done because fisherpeople protested against sea otters taking so many shellfish. There was also a fear that the small remaining population of sea otters could be wiped out by an oil spill.

Otters that strayed into the zone were captured and taken back north of Point Conception. In addition, about 100 sea otters were moved to a new habitat near San Nicolas Island, off the Southern California coast. However, most otters did not stay or breed there and returned to their original habitat.

A plan for southern sea otters was released in 2003. This plan aimed to monitor sea otter numbers, reduce the risk and effects of oil spills, and prevent any hunting of sea otters.

As a result, sea otters moved to Southern California again. Scientists and conservationists argued that an increase in the numbers of sea otters and the expansion of their habitat would result in more tourism and other related jobs in Southern California. The area's environment would also improve if the coastal ecosystem were healthier.

Only time will tell whether these creatures can continue to successfully survive in coastal areas with a large population and various industries.

▼ Sea otters live in shallow coastal waters off the northern Pacific Ocean.

## Other endangered marine mammals
- Blue whale
- Fin whale
- Gulf of California harbor porpoise
- Steller sea lion

▲ Manatee

▲ Humpback whale

▲ Hawaiian monk seal

# Chapter 5

# Reducing habitat destruction

The number of people in the world continues to grow. With this comes an increased need to use land for food, houses and services and the sea for food and recreation. These human needs will continue to destroy **habitats** and create problems for the survival of some **species**. The destruction of habitat needs to be balanced by the **conservation** and re-creation of suitable habitats for **endangered** animals.

Many endangered animals are now monitored and conservation programs are put into place to save them. Governments and international groups have put huge amounts of money and effort into saving endangered animals.

Education programs are provided by zoos, wildlife research centres, animal **refuges**, national parks and **World Heritage Sites**. As a result, people understand more about the needs of these animals, what is being done to save them from **extinction**, and how people and animals can successfully share their environment.

# Glossary

**captive breeding** programs set up by zoos and other centres to enable a group of animals to breed successfully

**captivity** being enclosed in a space

**conservation** preserving and protecting natural resources from destruction

**ecosystem** a whole community of living things that depend on each other for survival

**ecotourism** travel to natural areas to observe the wildlife and environment

**endangered** a plant or animal that may soon become extinct

**erodes** wears away

**extinct** when a species of plant or animal is no longer living on Earth

**habitat** any place where a plant or an animal naturally lives

**hatchlings** animals that have just hatched from eggs

**irrigation** water supply system made by humans for crop growing

**larvae** the young of insects that are hatched from eggs

**lobbied** talk to politicians to try to influence their decision-making

**mammals** animals that are warm-blooded, usually have hair, and give birth to live young that are fed on milk

**marine** belonging to the sea

**pelts** animal skins

**pesticides** chemicals used by people to kill pests such as insects

**population** the number of people, plants or animals in a group, country or species

**predators** animals that kill and eat other animals

**prey** an animal caught and eaten by another animal

**reforesting** planting new trees

**refuges** places that offer protection from harm or danger

**sanctuaries** places of safety for sick, abandoned or endangered animals

**species** a group of very closely related animals that can reproduce with each other

**territory** an area that an animal sees as its own

**vegetation** the plants that cover an area of land

**World Heritage Sites** places of world significance

# Index